PIANO LESSONS
FROM
CLASSICAL REPERTOIRE

20 Intermediate to Early Advanced Pieces
With Practice and Performance Tips

Selected and Edited by Immanuela Gruenberg

ISBN 978-1-5400-6865-1

Visit Hal Leonard Online at
www.halleonard.com

Contact us:
Hal Leonard
7777 West Bluemound Road
Milwaukee, WI 53213
Email: info@halleonard.com

In Europe, contact:
Hal Leonard Europe Limited
42 Wigmore Street
Marylebone, London, W1U 2RN
Email: info@halleonardeurope.com

In Australia, contact:
Hal Leonard Australia Pty. Ltd.
4 Lentara Court
Cheltenham, Victoria, 3192 Australia
Email: info@halleonard.com.au

ABOUT THIS COLLECTION

This publication is intended for teachers, students (intermediate to early-advanced levels), and piano connoisseurs. A number of considerations guided me in selecting the twenty compositions that comprise this publication: periodic/stylistic versatility; variety of technical and artistic levels; wide range of moods and characters; covering or introducing as many technical issues as possible; including an assortment of musical-artistic concepts. I also opted to include well-known and well-loved pieces along with lesser-known ones.

This collection includes works from the Baroque into the twentieth century by composers who were born or were active in Austria, Belgium-Netherlands, France, Germany, Hungary, Italy, Norway, Spain-Portugal, as well as the United States.

Some of the technical and musical concepts that this collection addresses are:

- Scales
- Arpeggios
- Chords (small and large ones; played *staccato* and *legato*, etc.)
- Octaves
- Double sixths and double thirds
- Touch: *staccato*, *legato*, *portato*, non-*legato*, *tenuto*, accents, *sf*
- Articulation
- Trills, turns, grace notes
- Fast runs
- Leaps
- Repeated notes

- Alberti bass
- *Glissando*
- Hand-over-hand crossing
- Lateral hand movement
- Lines transferred hand-to-hand
- *Cantabile* tone
- Multiple layers
- Melody and accompaniment
- Dynamics: *ppp* to *fff*
- Evenness of tone, touch, and timing
- Tempi: very fast to very slow
- Moods: cheerful, serious, somber, aggressive, gentle, sarcastic

My hope is that pianists will find here the kind of compositions they are looking for, as well as some pleasant surprises.

—Immanuela Gruenberg

CONTENTS

PIANO LESSONS

Carl Philipp Emanuel Bach: Solfeggietto in C Minor (H. 220)

This is a favorite among students, teachers, and amateurs.

AT A GLANCE

- The piece consists mainly of scale and broken-chord/arpeggio patterns.

- With few exceptions, this is a single-line piece, divided between the two hands.

PRACTICE AND PERFORMANCE TIPS

- Start with a group of notes played by one hand (for example, C–E-flat–G played by the left hand in m. 1, beat 1). Play these notes plus the first note that is played by the other hand. Gradually add more notes, all the while making sure to connect the hands seamlessly.

- Reverse the process: start with a group of notes further along the piece and "back up," starting with one, two, or more notes that precede this group. Keep adding notes in that manner.

- When deciding how to shape the lines, take into account the following:

- The shape created by the various pitches (think "connect the dots" game)
  - direction of the sequences
  - harmonic colors
  - harmonic progressions
  - harmonic rhythm, and
  - articulation.

- Pay attention to evenness of both tone and timing.

- Take into account that, for the most part, this is a single-line piece that could be played, for example, on a string instrument. Can you "hear" how this would sound on the violin or viola? Can you imagine the bowing? This can inspire your articulation.

Béla Bartók: Minuet (*The First Term at the Piano*)

Bartok composed *The First Term at the Piano* as a collection of pedagogy pieces. All the fingerings, dynamics, accents, tempo and metronome markings are by the composer. There are no editorial comments or suggestions in the score.

AT A GLANCE

- Very specific interpretive indications, especially as related to tone and touch

- *Grazioso* — specific character suggestion

- Two-note slurs

- Relatively narrow dynamic range: $\boldsymbol{p}$ to $\boldsymbol{mf}$

PRACTICE AND PERFORMANCE TIPS

- Use wrist *staccato* for the *grazioso* character and required touch.

- Note that in spite of the *crescendos*, it never gets louder than $\boldsymbol{mf}$.

- While playing a series of *staccatos*, change the height of the wrist. This helps shape the line while also relaxing the wrist.

Domenico Cimarosa: Sonata in B-flat Major (C. 27)

This light-hearted sonata features a variety of pianistic and musical elements characteristic of Classical-era style.

AT A GLANCE

- Alberti bass (in both the left- and right-hand parts)

- Hand-over-hand crossings

- Easy tremolos

- Turns

- Some surprising modulations

- Numerous opportunities for echo effects

- Overall clear texture

PRACTICE AND PERFORMANCE TIPS

- The touch should be mostly non-*legato*.

- For variety, you may occasionally use two-note slurs, such as on the first beat in measures 5, 6, etc. When this motive reappears, you may want to play these notes detached.

- Note the parallel thirds and sixths created between the Alberti and the eighths notes (mm. 11, 12, etc.)

- Alberti figures and sixteenths notes: use very soft, light thumbs whether played by the left or by the right hand.

- Practice tips for the Alberti: measures 5–6, for example: place the thumb on the F, holding the key down with as little weight as possible while playing the other notes—B-flat, D in measure 5 and A, C in measure 6—with an articulated touch and very slight rotation of the hand. Then play as written, keeping the thumb soft, light, and close to the key.

- When hands play close to one another, figure out the angle of each hand and the height of each wrist. Experiment with different angles and wrist heights to find the ones that work best for you.

Gabriel Fauré: Romance Without Words in A-flat Major (Op. 17 No. 3)

A beautiful, lyrical piece that incorporates a singing right-hand part with left-hand accompaniment played with lateral motion.

AT A GLANCE

- Lyrical melody on top and left-hand accompaniment

- The accompaniment consists of two layers: the quarter-note bass notes and the arpeggiated chords.

- Around the middle of the piece, an echo is added to the melody.

PRACTICE AND PERFORMANCE TIPS

- Play the right-hand part along with only the left-hand downbeats to hear both lines without the rest of the left-hand notes.

- Focus on the quick yet gentle pedal change on the downbeats, making sure to catch each downbeat in a new, clean pedal, without any accents or harsh releases of pedal or of keys.

- While the bass notes need to be released quickly in order for the thumb to reach the second sixteenth, the release should never be abrupt. These downbeats should never sound *staccato* or accented.

- Opt for long lines in the right hand. These melodic lines should not be influenced by the left-hand's repetitive, single-measure rhythmic pattern.

- Dotted rhythms often have a tendency to sound rhythmic. This should not happen with the melodic line, which should sound melodic, never "angular."

- In measures 41–55, where the right-hand part includes an echo of the melody, Fauré changes the notation of the bass. Consider playing this bass line differently from how you play elsewhere in the piece.

- Measure 49–53: the suggested fingering divides the middle voice part between the two hands. You could, however, play this voice with only the right hand. In that case, it is important to decide: Do you play the alto on the beat and the soprano slightly later, or do you play the soprano on the beat with the alto preceding it? Personally, I prefer the first option which adds some subtle flexibility. Either way, the beat should remain steady.

César Franck: Adagio (*Three Early Pieces*)

This little piece has much in common with its more mature cousins, the Chopin nocturnes.

AT A GLANCE:

- A melodic, *cantabile* top

- Accompaniment that consists of low bass notes followed by *arpeggio*/broken chord notes

- Minor variations, such as embellishments of the melody (compare, for example, mm. 3–4 to mm. 11–12) are written out in large notes

PRACTICE AND PERFORMANCE TIPS

- The left-hand part should be played mostly with a flat hand and flat fingers. Play with the cushiony part of the fingers and move the hand laterally.

- Even though Franck does not mark the right-hand "*legato*," it is implied by the "*cantabile*."

- Left Hand: when moving from the downbeat octave to the next note, have the hand pivot around the thumb, moving it laterally. In other words, start moving the left part of your hand toward the thumb before releasing the thumb. That said, be sure to not play the bass note *staccato*!

- Note the different shapes of the left-hand *arpeggios*. Shape the lines accordingly.

- Right Hand: practice it very slowly, transferring the weight from one finger to the next, using more weight on some notes and less on others according to the shape of the phrase.

- Try to combine two- and four-measure phrases to create longer lines. For example, measures 1–2 form a single, short unit as do measure 3–4. These two units can—and should—be combined to create a longer one, with measures 3–4 slightly more expressive than 1–2 because of their higher pitches. Keep working in that manner to create long lines.

César Franck: Poco maestoso (*L'organiste*, Volume 1)

This piece was originally written for the harmonium, a fact that is evident in its texture.

AT A GLANCE

- A unique texture: the four layers are divided between the two hands so that each hand plays two layers in unison with the other hand's two layers.

- Throughout the piece there are sustained notes and chords while other voices move.

PRACTICE AND PERFORMANCE TIPS

- The sustained notes are characteristic of the harmonium. Listen to how they sound and how they interact with all the other notes. Pay special attention to measures 5, 6, 7, etc. and listen to how the notes played on the second beat blend with the sustained ones.

- Play as *legato* as possible.

- Try to create long, 8-measure lines.

- Once you have played a note that has to be sustained, use the minimum weight necessary to keep that key down. For example: once you've played the first E-flats *forte*, keep only minimal weight on the left-hand thumb and the right-hand fifth finger, while continuing to play *f* the rest of the notes (bass and alto).

Edvard Grieg: Bell Ringing (*Lyric Pieces*, Op. 54, No. 6)

The title of the piece is unambiguous, telling the listener and performer that the main feature of this piece is sound. The piece is quite easy to read and to learn with the main difficulty being tone and control of dynamics.

AT A GLANCE

- With the exception of the last few measures, the (very simple) rhythm stays the same throughout. Likewise, with few exceptions, the open fifth intervals are a constant feature.

PRACTICE AND PERFORMANCE TIPS

- Given the steady, repetitive rhythm and musical material, structure, tension, and drama are achieved by means of tone, harmonic colors and dynamics.

- Listen to Grieg's *Lyric Suite* which includes the composer's orchestrated version of this piece.

- Plan your dynamics: play the *ppp* parts as softly as possible, then play the *fff* measures. These are your dynamic boundaries. They enable you to plan the rest of the dynamics within these dynamic limits.

- Right Hand: Note the difference between notes with *tenuto* markings and those without.

- Practice and compare the two different touches, leaning into the keys on the *tenuto* notes.

Franz Joseph Haydn: Allegretto (Sonata in C Major, Hob. XVI:3)

A delightful *allegretto* in C major that features many of Haydn's characteristics while also being easy to learn and not too hard to play.

AT A GLANCE

- Left Hand: simple, repetitive broken chords within a range no wider than a sixth

- Right Hand: Short scale patterns

- Trills and turns

PRACTICE AND PERFORMANCE TIPS

- Practice the left-hand part as blocked chords, holding each one down for as long as the notes stay the same. This should help with memory and also draw your attention to the various harmonic progressions.

- Use a light touch and slight rotation from the fifth finger to the thumb.

- The ornaments may consist of fewer or more notes, depending on your technical ability and on the tempo you choose. The touch should be crisp and clear.

- Always play the left hand softer than the right hand.

- The default touch is non-*legato*.

Franz Liszt: Etude in D Minor (Op. 1, No. 4)

Composed in 1826 when Liszt was only fifteen, the *Etudes*, Op.1 became the basis of what Liszt eventually turned into his *Transcendental Etudes*.

AT A GLANCE

- Double thirds

- Hand-over-hand crossings

- Use of much of the piano's keyboard—close to six octaves

PRACTICE AND PERFORMANCE TIPS

- Without actually playing, place each hand in turn on the keys it has to play so you can better master these hand crossings. This applies to measures 1–24, 41–56, and 65–74. Start slowly and work up to tempo.

- Always look ahead to where the hand has to move. While playing with one hand look to where the other hand is moving next so you can get it there on time.

- Note that the double thirds are written almost exclusively in a five-finger position.

- In each group of thirds (or thirds and fourths, as in mm. 17, 18, etc.) practice the top notes *legato* while separating the bottom notes. Then reverse.

- Practice the top lines alone and the bottom ones alone, always making sure to use correct fingering.

- Make sure the double thirds (and occasional fourth) are always struck together.

Edward MacDowell: The Witch (*Marionettes*, Op. 38, No. 6)

AT A GLANCE

- Chords

- Crisp, marked *staccatos*

- A wide dynamic range

- Marked rhythms (including double dotted notes)

- A delicate *glissando* rounding off the drama

PRACTICE AND PERFORMANCE TIPS

- When you start the piece *mf,* as marked, remember to leave room for *f* and *ff!*

- Carefully observe the few, short *legato* instances. These act as contrast to the sharp *staccatos*.

- Try voicing the top notes, for clarity and crispness of sound.

- When practicing *staccatos* slowly, the slow tempo should only apply to the time *between* notes/chords, not to the time you spend *on* each note or chord. In other words, even in a slow tempo the *staccato* notes should be short, and the hands should move quickly to the next chord.

- The sharp *staccato* notes should be played with strong fingers and active fingertips. Think *pizzicato*, especially when it comes to the top notes.

Felix Mendelssohn: Prelude in B-flat Major (Op. 35, No. 6)

This is the sixth of Mendelssohn's *Six Preludes and Fugues*, composed between 1827 and 1837.

AT A GLANCE

- Chords are the basis of both the melody and the accompaniment of this prelude.

- The accompaniment chords move mostly upward.

- Both hands play both the melody and the accompaniment.

PRACTICE AND PERFORMANCE TIPS

- Think two beats per measure.

- Be sure to maintain continuity and structure of the slow-moving melodic line.

- Create and maintain consistency of sound in the lines composed, intermittently, of chords, octaves, and single notes.

- Strive for smooth transitions from one chord/position to the next.

- On repeated notes or chords (mm. 4, 9, 12, etc.), keep the line moving forward, leading to the next note or beat.

- To voice the chords that are part of the melodic line, lean on the finger playing the top note and use less weight on the other fingers. Practice this by leaning with the weight of your hand and arm on the top note, and play lightly, slowly, and repeatedly the other notes of the chord.

- Practice top notes only, both on their own and with the accompaniment, in order to get a good feel of the melodic line and to hear it clearly.

- When the right hand plays some of the accompaniment chords in addition to the melody, make sure to play these accompaniment chords with the tone, character, and dynamics of the ones played by the left hand.

Felix Mendelssohn:
A Song Without Words in F Major

Dedicated to *Fräulein* Doris Loewe, this is a stand-alone piece, not one of the forty-eight *Songs Without Words* that were published as sets.

This is a great introductory piece to more advanced *Songs Without Words* and to multi-layered pieces in general.

AT A GLANCE

- Three distinct layers: a bass line, a melodic line on top, and an inner arpeggiated/broken-chord accompaniment

- *Legato*

- *Cantabile*

- Shaping of phrases

PRACTICE AND PERFORMANCE TIPS

- Practice each layer separately, paying attention to each layer's tone, touch, character, etc. While each layer should have its own distinct tone, touch, and shape, they all have to work together.

- Practice all possible two-layer combinations.

- Practice hands separately, paying special attention to instances where two layers are played, simultaneously, by the same hand.

- Bass: use an even, steady, *tenuto* touch. Listen to the harmonic line.

- Arpeggiated middle layer: Make the hand-to-hand transfer a smooth one. Shape each *arpeggio* (while also paying attention to the overall melodic and harmonic structure. Practice it as blocked chords, alone and with the bass, to get a better feel for the harmonic lines and colors. This layer should be played softer than the outer two.

- Top line: this should be played *legato* and with a singing tone.

Leopold Mozart:
Allegro moderato in F Major
(*Nannerl's Notebook*)

A fun piece, easy to learn and to play while being very beneficial technically, musically, and stylistically.

AT A GLANCE

- Alberti bass, alternating between the hands and thus not always a "bass"

- Rapid hand crossings: These are the technical manifestations of the piece's musical idea of a dialogue.

PRACTICE AND PERFORMANCE TIPS

- Left-Hand Alberti: make sure the thumb is light and plays softly, as these repeated notes fall on the weakest part of the beat.

- Right-Hand Alberti: light thumb when it plays repeated notes (mm. 5–6, 7–8, etc.); more tone but still articulated, when playing a line (mm. 9–10, etc.)

- The default touch here is non-*legato*.

- Use a very small, gentle, *tremolo* (back and forth) motion.

- Occasional *legato* may be used on the melody notes for special effect.

- To practice the leaps, hold the stationary hand in place while focusing on the leaps only. Always look ahead of time to where you have to move the hand.

Wolfgang Amadeus Mozart: German Dance in E-flat Major (K. 509, No. 3)

A lively, short piece, that seems longer due to the repeats and the ABA, *da capo*, form. It is suitable for teaching and practicing various *arpeggio* positions, Alberti bass, double thirds, and contrasting moods: part A is energetic and lively while part B is soft and lyrical.

AT A GLANCE

- Evenness of right-hand broken chords/*arpeggios* sixteenths

- Moving the hand from one position to another and changing fingers in the process

- Left-Hand Alberti: Even sixteenths and soft thumb

PRACTICE AND PERFORMANCE TIPS

- Note that as you move from one broken-chord position to the next, you may play the same key with different fingers. Look, for example, at measures 1–2. The right-hand E-flat is played first with the fourth finger, then the third and after that, the second. Practice this by playing measure 1 stopping on the first note, E-flat, in measure 2. Then stop on the third note in measure 2, the E-flat played by the second finger. Focus on these transitions: measures 9–14, right hand on the repeated chords, lead to the following down beat. Slightly adjusting the height of your wrist on each of these chords helps to create a line, a sense of direction.

- Always strive for long lines.

- Double thirds, measures 17–24 and 29–32 play as *legato* as possible the top notes of the right hand and the bottom notes of the left hand. Practice each of these "voices" on their own, then add the thirds. Keep the thumbs light and relaxed.

Erik Satie: Crooked Dance No. 2 (*Cold Pieces*)

Easy to read and quite easy to play, this piece nevertheless features some surprises.

AT A GLANCE

- No meter, no bar-lines, and no apparent ending

- Somewhat free flowing

- Constant interaction between left and right hand and between melody and accompaniment

- Other ideas repeated throughout: ascending broken chords; eighths notes

PRACTICE AND PERFORMANCE TIPS

- Pay attention to the repetitive musical ideas: rhythm (eighth notes throughout), melodic line, accompaniment (ascending four-note broken chord), vs. the subtle changes to the melody, color (single notes vs. octaves), and the more pronounced harmonic changes.

- Practice the accompaniment by itself—both as written and as blocked chords—and the melody by itself.

- Put the two together, paying special attention the double-stemmed notes that do double duty, belonging to both the accompaniment and the melody.

- Experiment with very subtle *rubatos* and timing/breaths in between the phrases.

- If you're playing this piece by itself, not as part of the set of three *Cold Pieces*, slow down towards the end to give a sense of an ending

Domenico Scarlatti: Sonata C Major (K. 95/L. 358)

This sonata is easy to read, easy to learn, and fun to play.

AT A GLANCE

- Suitable for small hands: there are no chords and only one instance in which the left hand covers a range larger than a sixth.
- The right hand plays almost exclusively single notes.
- Left Hand: Alberti bass
- Right Hand: leaps
- Right hand crossing over the left hand
- Short trills

PRACTICE AND PERFORMANCE TIPS

- This piece can be played *moderato*, perhaps with the left hand detached throughout and with a lighthearted, even humorous, mood. It can also be played fast with a focus on the right-hand "acrobatics" and on brilliant-sounding trills.
- Because the left hand is confined to a small area around middle C, the student can easily focus on the right-hand leaps.
- Think of the right-hands' contrasting registers in terms of different orchestral instruments and contrasting dynamics.
- As is always the case with repeats, use them to make some changes—in touch, dynamics, ornamentation, articulation, etc.
- Left hand: pay attention to evenness of tone and timing.
- Use slight wrist rotation
- Practice the left hand as blocked chords, both alone and with the right hand. Listen to the harmony as you do so. This also helps with memorization.
- Hold the left hand in place without playing, while practicing the right-hand leaps.
- Divide the right-hand part between the two hands, playing the bass notes with the left hand. This will help you feel and hear the dialogue that's going on.

Domentico Scarlatti: Sonata in D Minor (K. 141/L. 422)

A brilliant, lively sonata, that is as fun to play as it is to listen to.

AT A GLANCE

- Repeated notes—one of the sonata's main technical (and musical) characteristics
- *Tremolos*
- *Arpeggios*
- Hand crossings

PRACTICE AND PERFORMANCE TIPS

- While touch and articulation in scale and arpeggio patterns may be different from those in repeated notes, they all should be played non-*legato*.
- The abundance of repeated notes should not interfere with shaping of lines and phrases. For example, in measures 1–8, use the right-hand pitches ("line") and left-hand harmony to better get a feel for the direction of the phrase.
- When repeating a part, experiment using different fingerings in order for them to sound subtly different. On repeated notes you may, for example, use fingers 4-3-2-1-2-1.
- Some left-hand chords, especially at the beginning of the piece, may be rolled.

Franz Schubert: Ecossaise in E-flat Major (D. 735, No. 3)

A short, lively, rhythmic, piece.

AT A GLANCE

- Very short piece—only eight measures!
- Within these 8 measures, a wide dynamic range: **p** to **ff**
- Double thirds
- Accents
- Short slurs
- Left-hand *staccato*

PRACTICE AND PERFORMANCE TIPS

- Approach the double thirds as two independent lines, or voices, and practice each one separately (with correct fingering!).

- Practice each group of thirds that fit within one hand position (five-finger position) on its own. For example, in measure 1, one of the groups is E-flat–G, D–F, C–E-flat, and the other is B-flat–D, A-flat–C, G–B-flat, F–A-flat. Make sure to play the two notes of each third at exactly the same moment.

- The next step would be to connect the above two groups, playing one group plus the first third of the second group. Then, play the last third of a group plus the entire second group. Finally, play the entire progression.

- When crossing over the thumb (C–E-flat to B-flat–D) move your hand laterally, parallel to the keyboard.

- Measures 5 and 7: the rhythm on the first beat suggests a kind of gesture that requires breathing and taking some time before the second eighths of the beat.

Franz Schubert:
Ländler in D-flat Major (D. 145, No. 7)

This lovely, 16-measure piece, presents excellent opportunities to study various pianistic skills.

AT A GLANCE

- Very short piece
- Trills
- Using the thumb on black keys
- Dotted rhythms
- Short slurs
- Delicate touches

PRACTICE AND PERFORMANCE TIPS

- Try different fingerings for the trills. Often, non-adjoining fingers, such as 1 and 3, 2 and 4, or 3 and 5, work best. Listen for speed of the trill but also for evenness of touch and timing.

- Note: the second and third beats in each measure should be played *p*.

- Notice, also, Schubert's very important articulations: only the second beat in each measure is marked *staccato* and is followed by a two-note slur.

- Since the right hand stays in one place during much of the piece you are free to look at the left hand to more easily control the leaps.

Robert Schumann: Wild Rider,
(*Album for the Young*, Op. 68 No. 8)

This is one of the most popular pieces from Schumann's *Album for the Young*.

AT A GLANCE

- Constant *staccato*, for both the right and the left hand
- Two-note slurs
- *sf*
- Chords

PRACTICE AND PERFORMANCE TIPS

- Practice slowly, however move the hand as quickly as possible from one note to the next.

- When playing these *staccatos*, think of moving the hand horizontally, along the keyboard, rather than up and down.

- This is an energetic piece, that should be played with constant forward drive.

- Always think of leading to the next beat, then lead to the downbeat of the following measure, which in many instances means leading to a *sf*.

- Same direction applies to the left hand: short *staccatos* eighths lead to the longer, non-*staccato* quarter note.

Solfeggietto in C Minor
H. 220

Carl Philipp Emanuel Bach
(1714–1788)

3

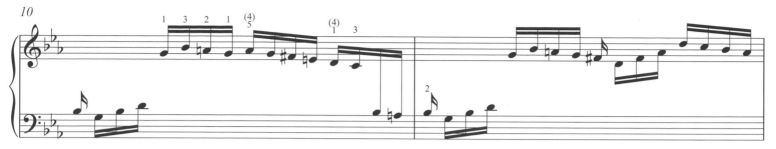

Minuet
The First Term at the Piano

Béla Bartók
(1881–1945)

* Fingerings by the composer.

Sonata in B-flat Major
C. 27

Domenico Cimarosa
(1749–1801)

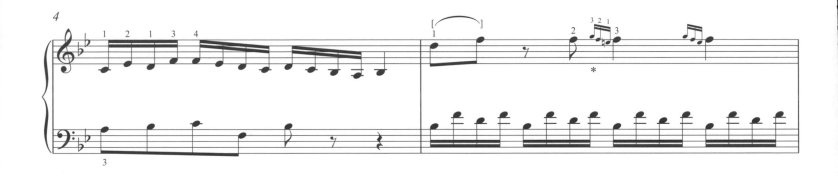

*The turns begin on the beat.

* G4 in some sources.
** B3 in some sources.

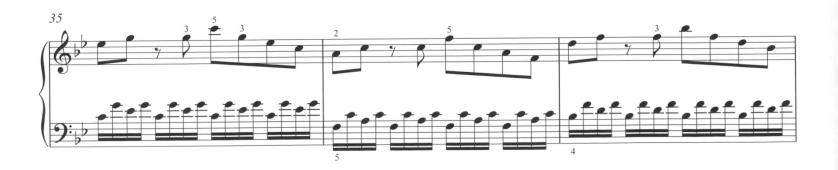

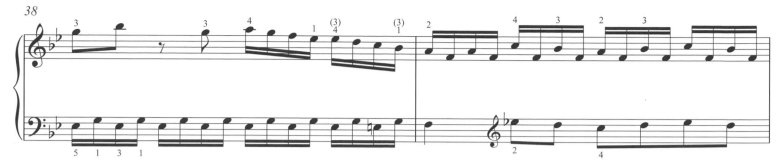

to Madame Florent Saglio

Romance Without Words in A-flat Major
Op. 17, No. 3

Gabriel Fauré
(1845–1924)

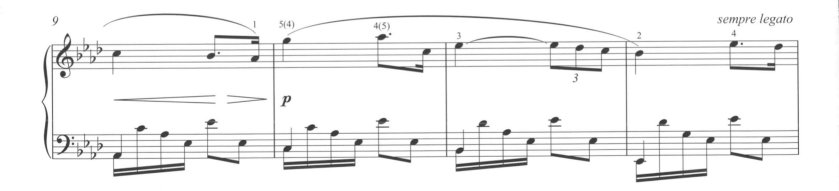

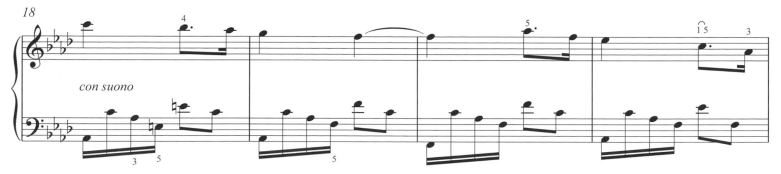

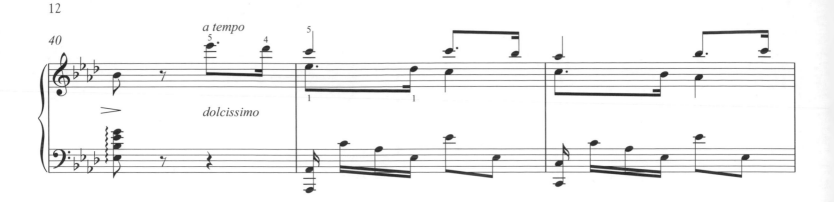

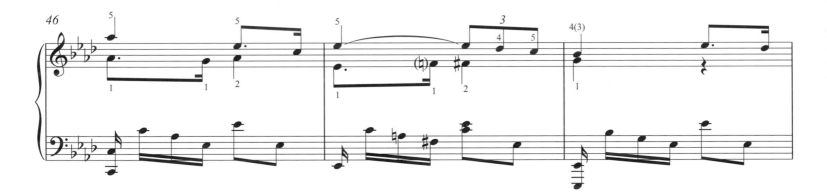

* See Practice Tips

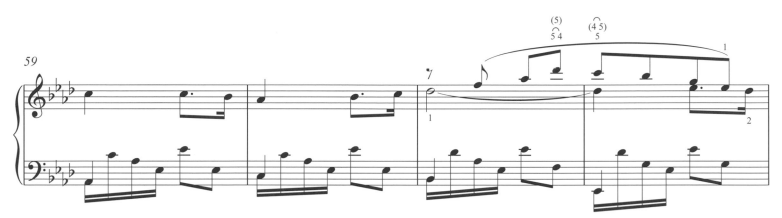

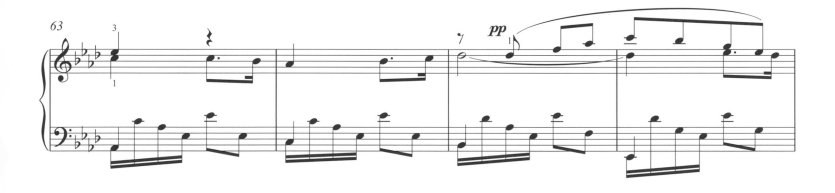

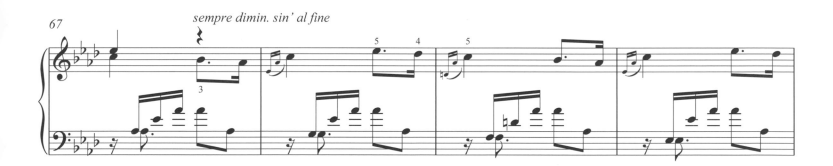

Adagio
Three Early Pieces

César Franck
(1822–1890)

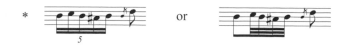

Poco maestoso

L'organiste, Volume 1

César Franck
(1822–1890)

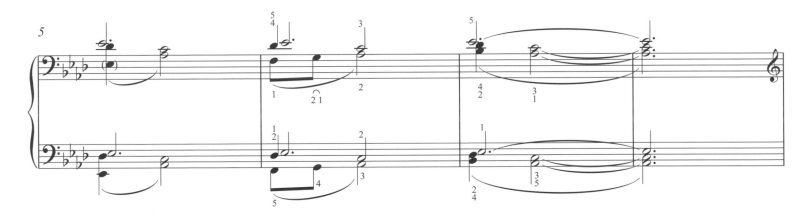

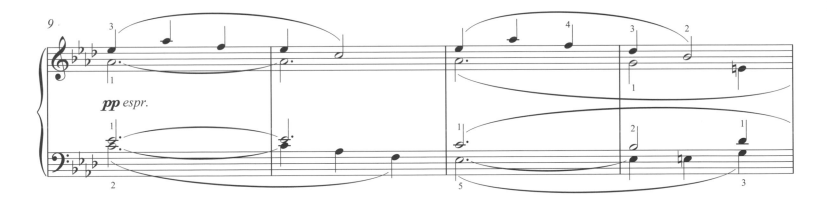

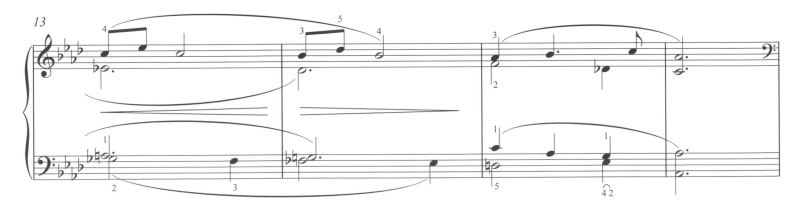

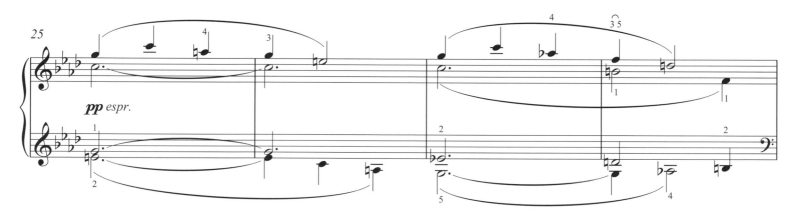

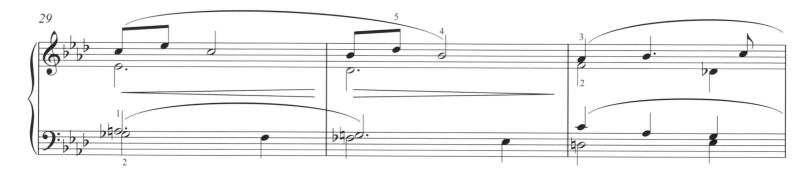

Piú lento

Bell Ringing
Lyric Pieces, Op. 54, No. 6

Edvard Grieg
(1843–1907)

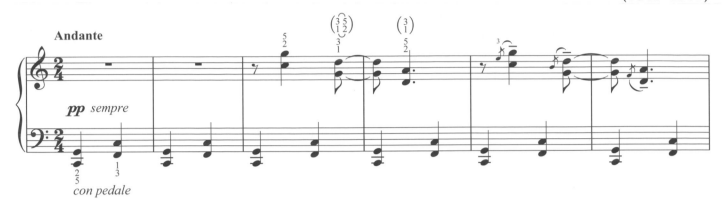

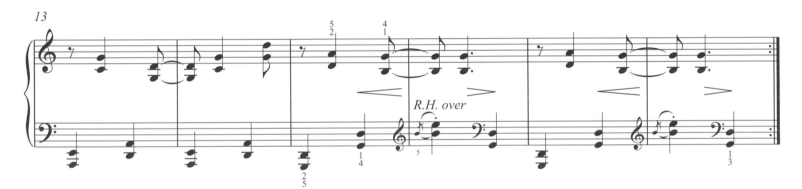

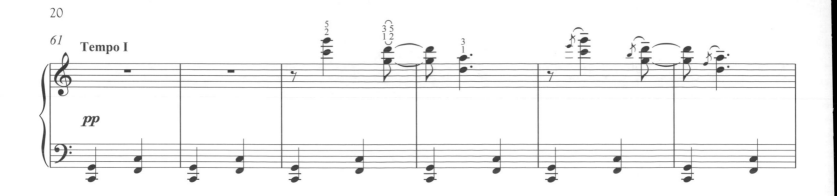

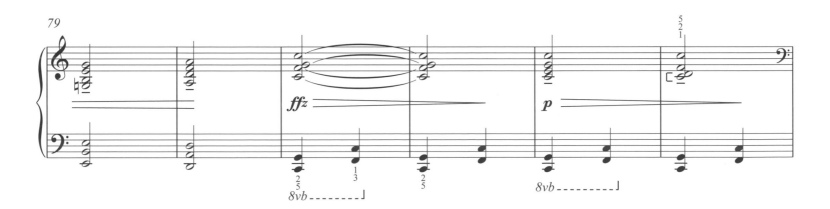

Allegretto
Sonata in C Major, Hob. XVI:3

Franz Joseph Haydn
(1732–1809)

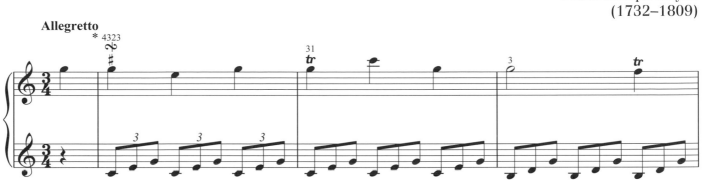

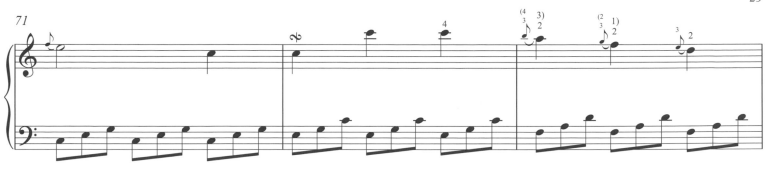

Etude in D Minor
Op. 1, No. 4

Franz Liszt
(1811–1886)

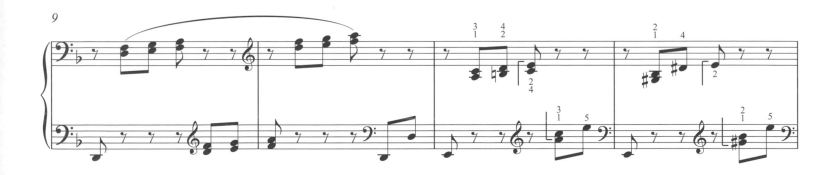

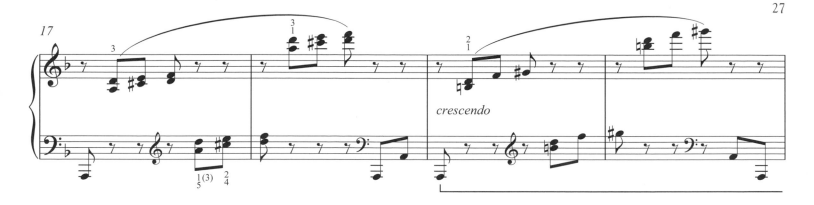

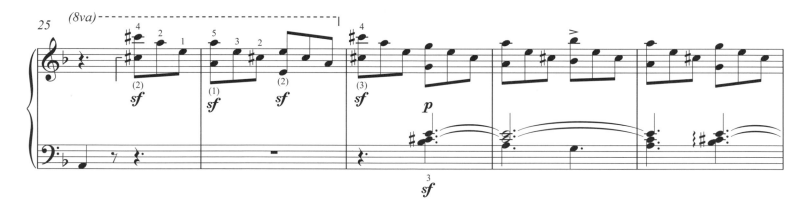

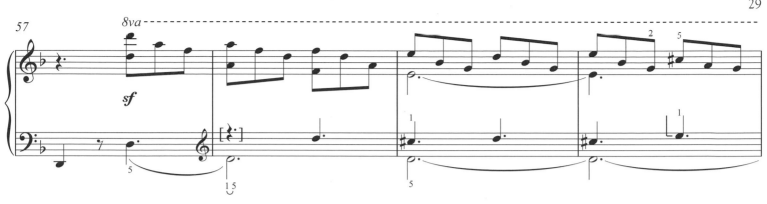

The Witch
Marionettes, Op. 38, No. 6

Edward MacDowell
(1860–1908)

With much character (♩ = c. 138)

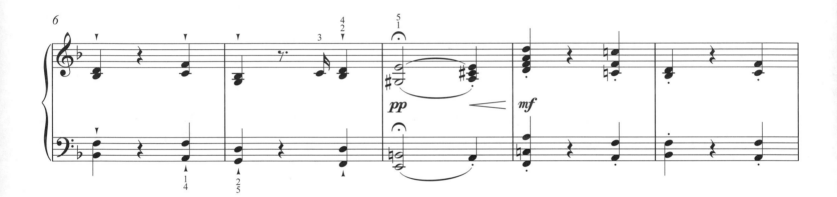

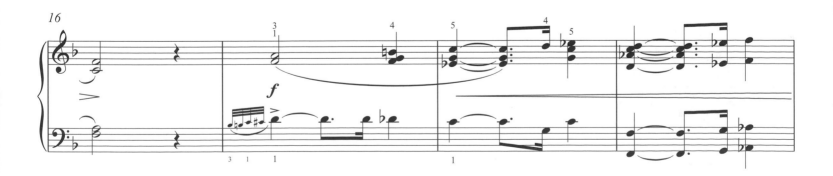

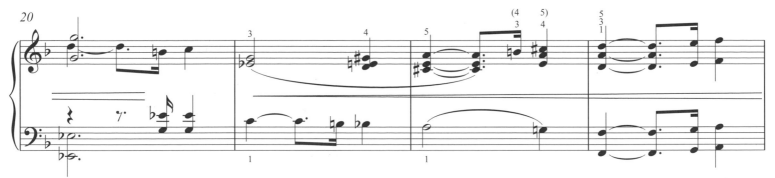

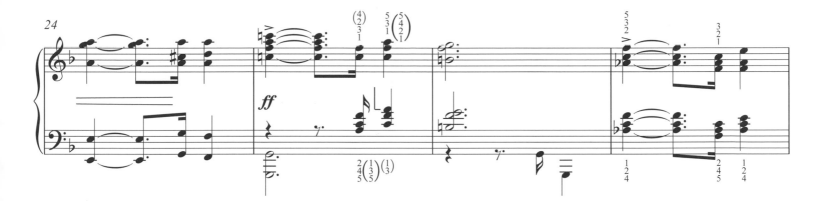

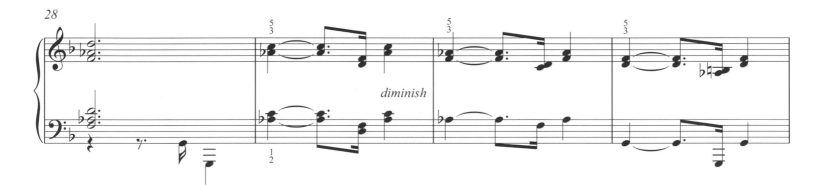

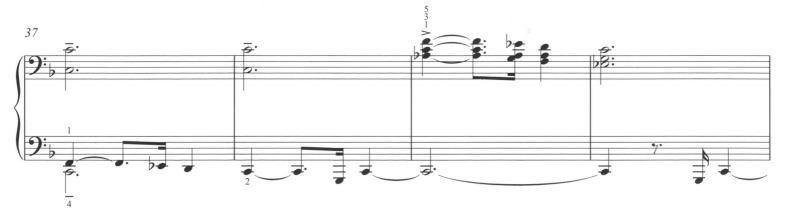

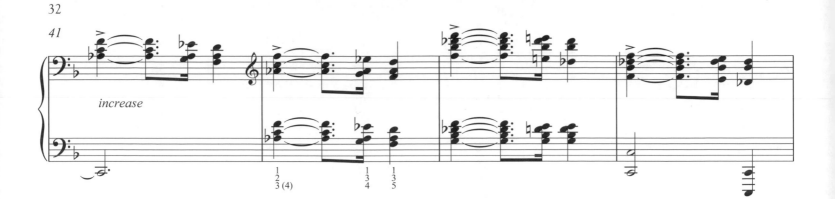

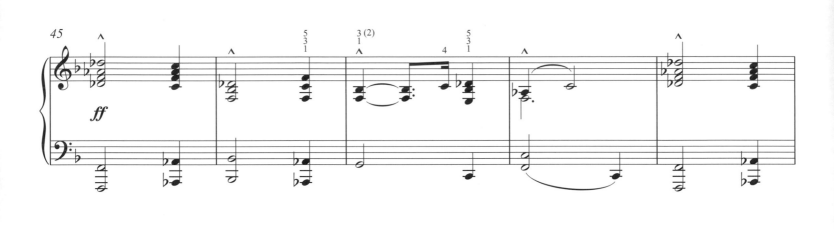

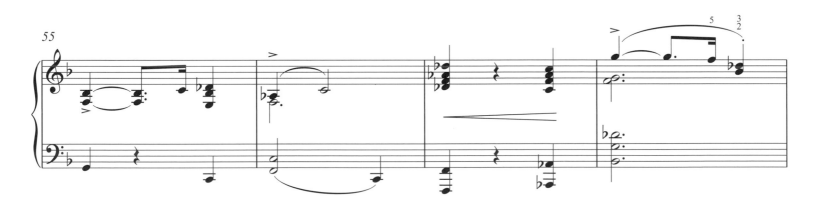

Prelude in B-flat Major
Op. 35, No. 6

Felix Mendelssohn
(1809–1847)

Maestoso moderato

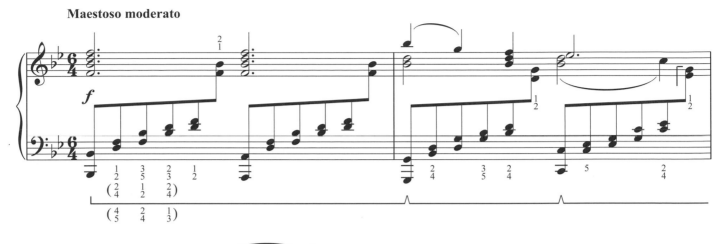

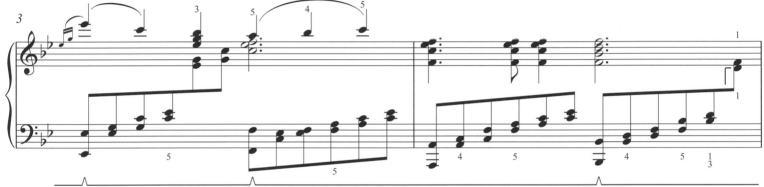

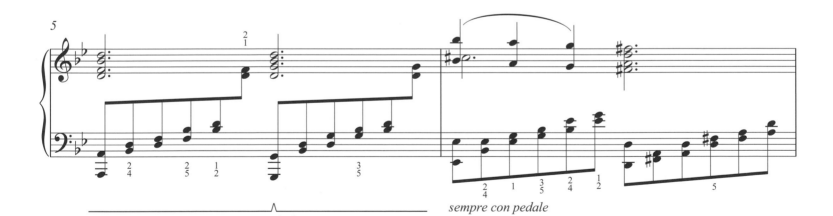

sempre con pedale

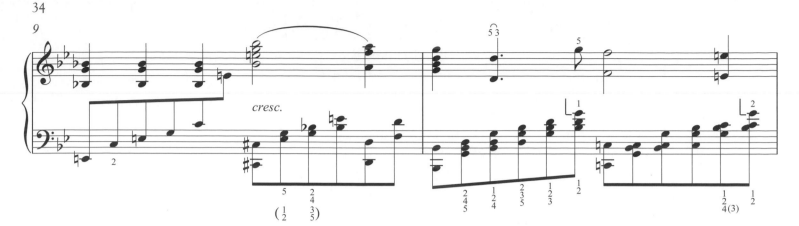

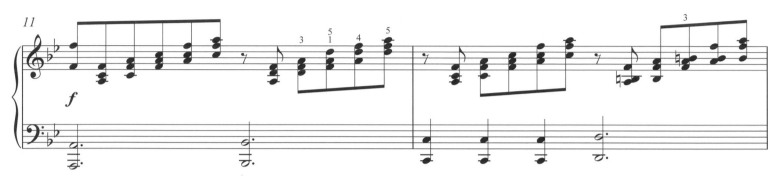

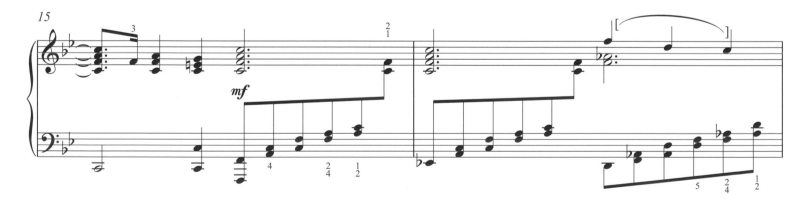

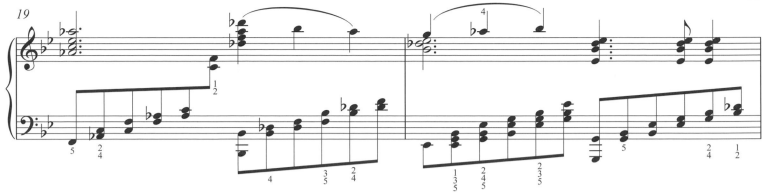

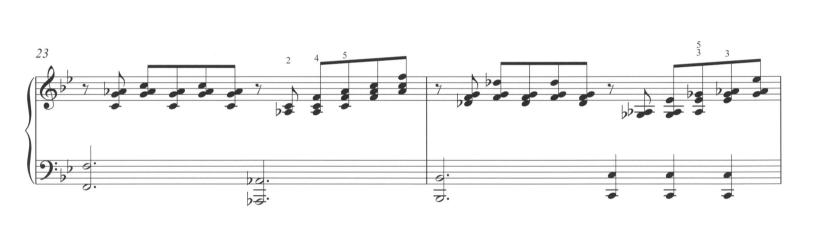

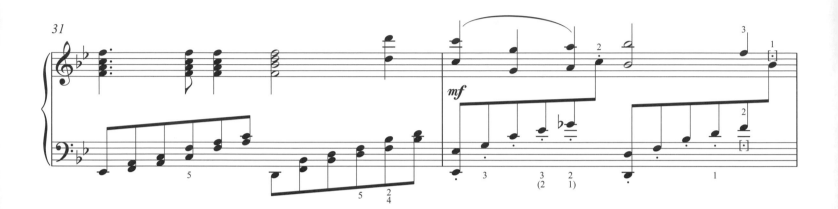

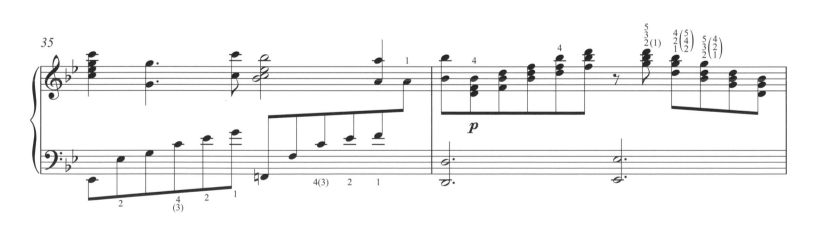

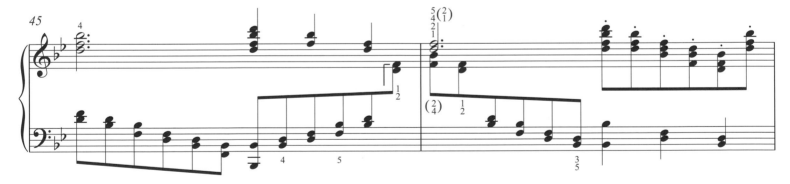

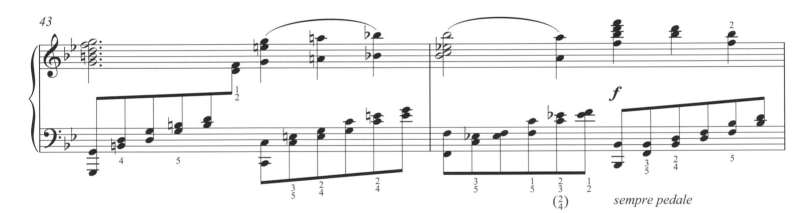

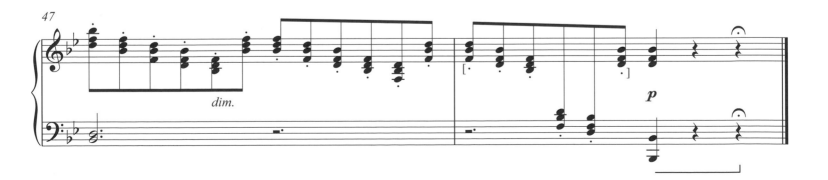

A Song Without Words in F Major

Felix Mendelssohn
(1809–1847)

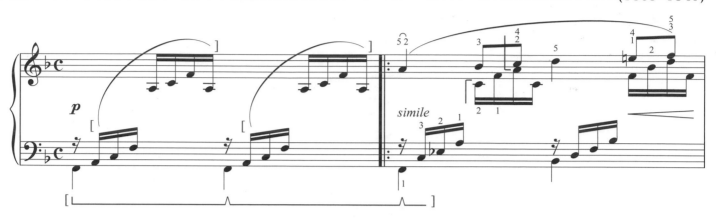

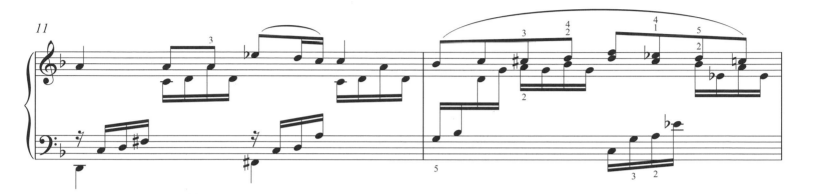

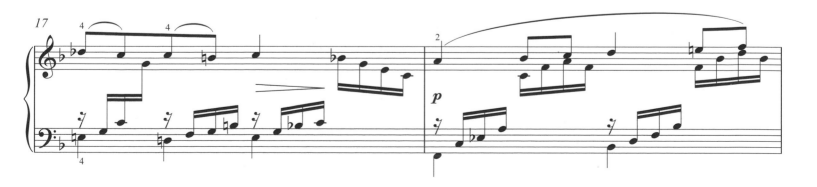

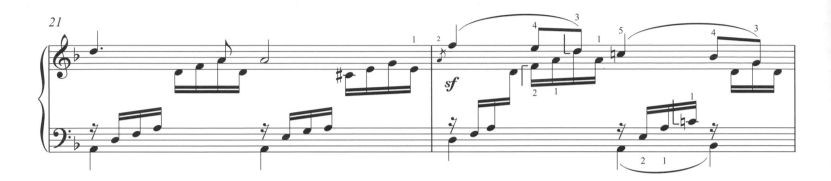

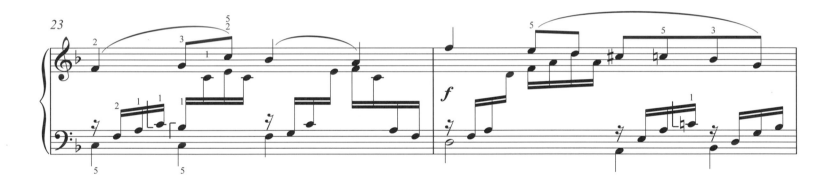

Allegro moderato in F Major

Nannerl's Notebook

Leopold Mozart
(1719–1787)

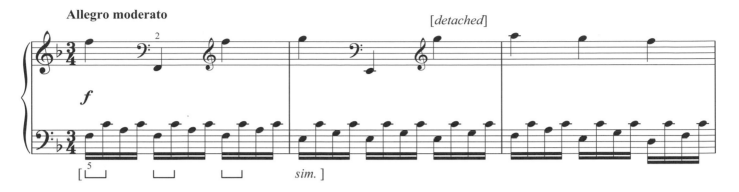

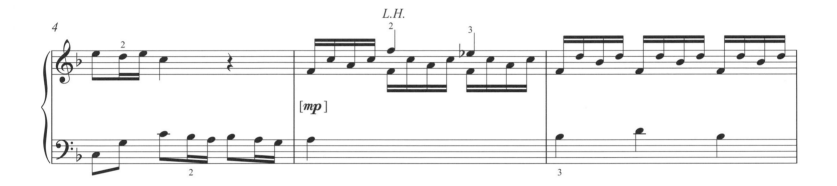

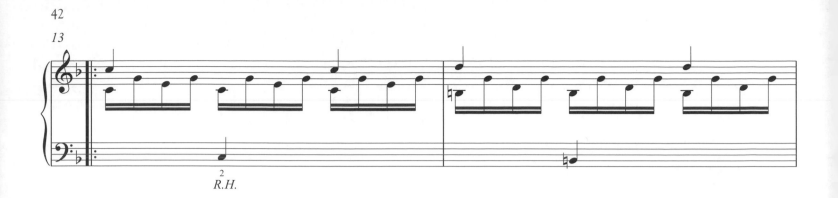

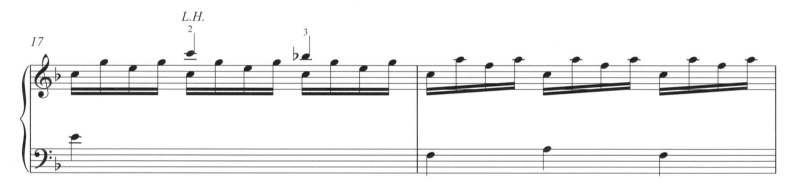

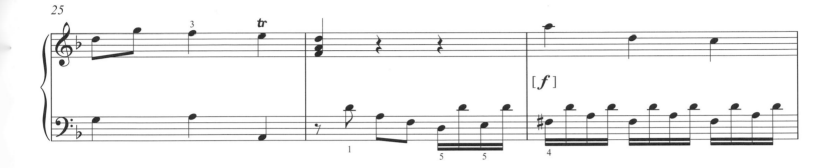

German Dance in E-flat Major

K. 509, No. 3

Wolfgang Amadeus Mozart
(1756–1791)

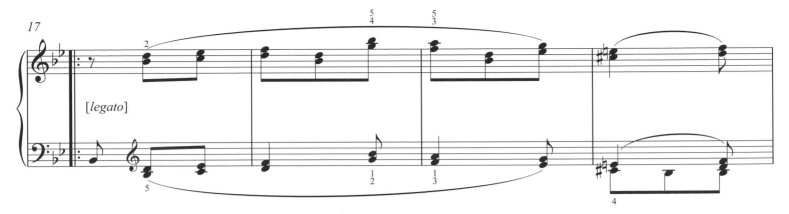

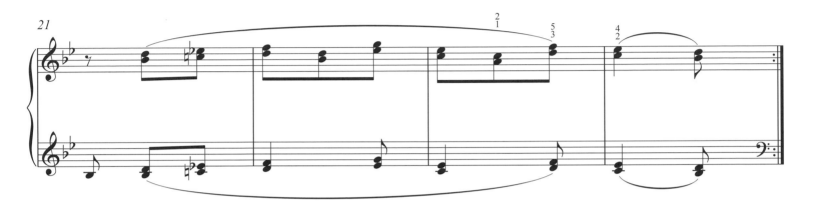

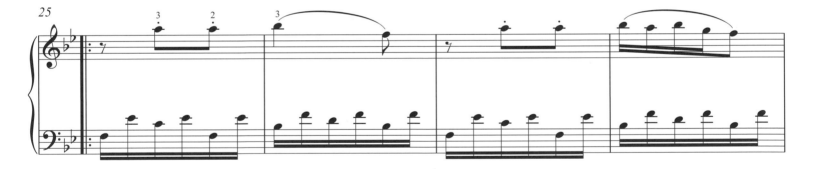

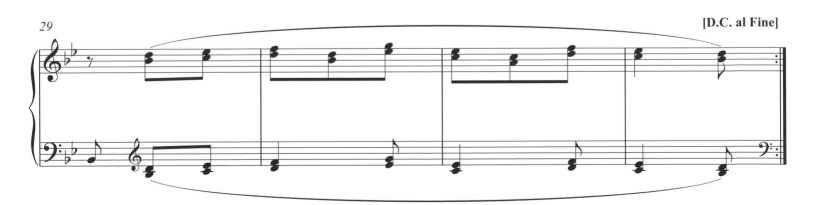

Crooked Dance No. 2

Cold Pieces

Erik Satie
(1866–1925)

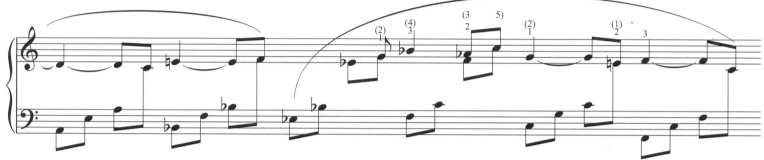

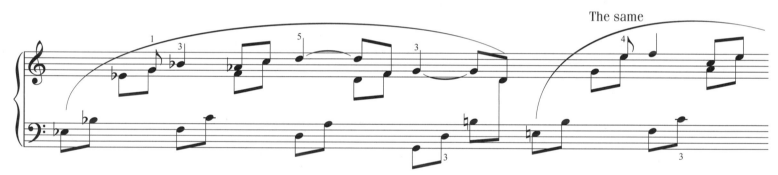

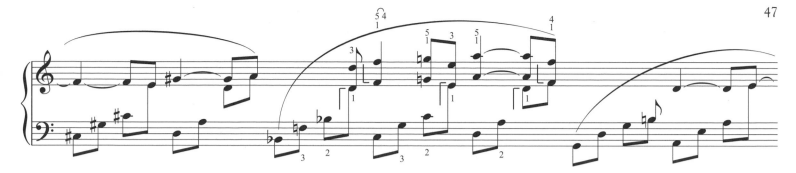

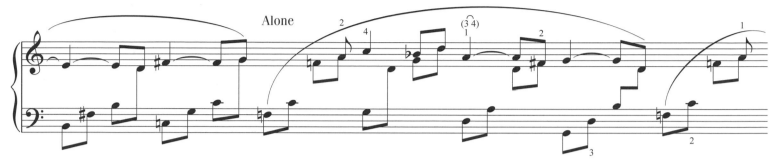

Alone

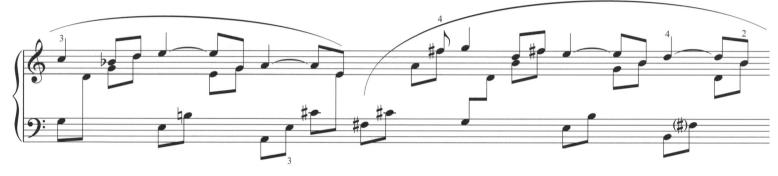

Be visible for a moment

Blend together

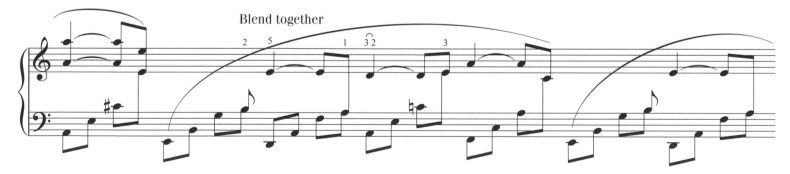

Medium done

Ecossaise in E-flat Major
D. 735, No. 3

Franz Schubert
(1797–1828)

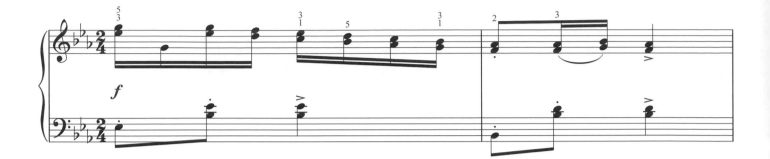

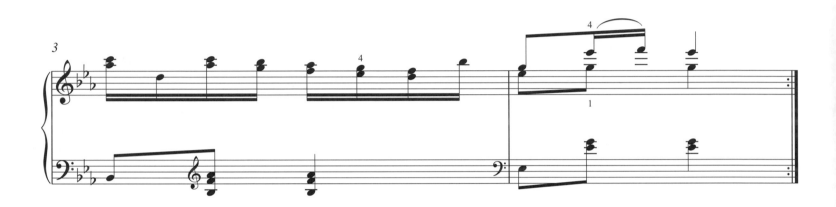

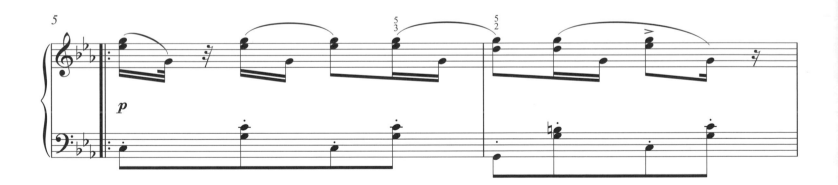

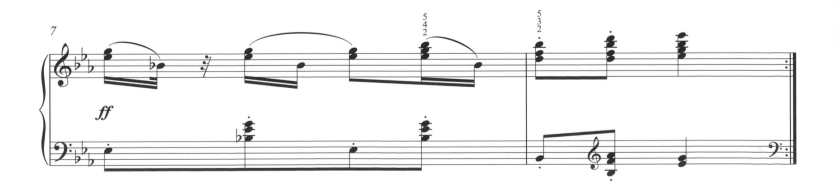

Ländler in D-flat Major
D. 145, No. 7

Franz Schubert
(1797–1828)

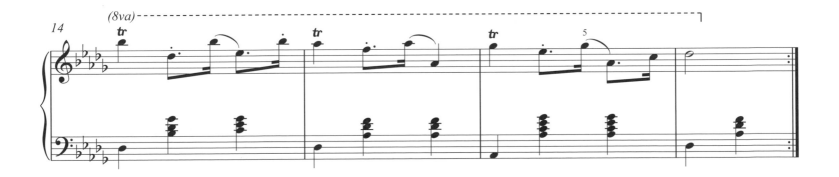

Wild Rider

Album for the Young, Op. 68, No. 8

Robert Schumann
(1810–1856)

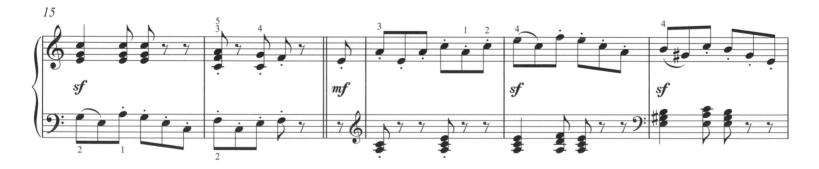

Sonata in D Minor
K. 141, L. 422

Domenico Scarlatti
(1685–1757)

Allegro

52

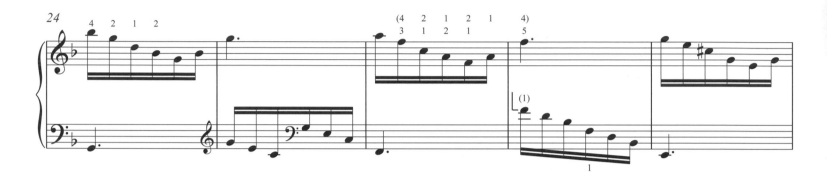

* F in some sources.

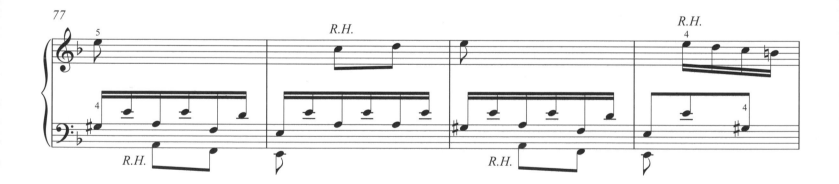

113

117

121

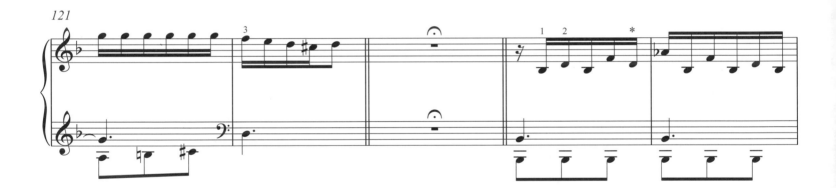

126

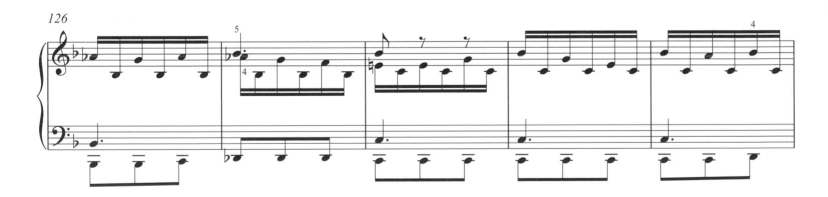

131

* B-flat in some sources.

Sonata in C Major
K. 95/ L. 358

Domenico Scarlatti
(1685–1757)

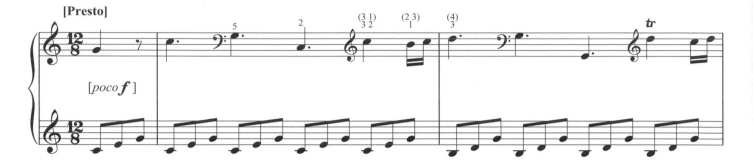

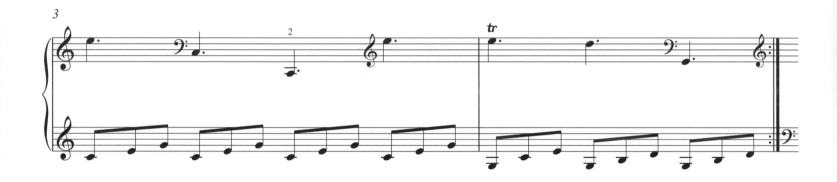

* Grace notes occur on the beat.